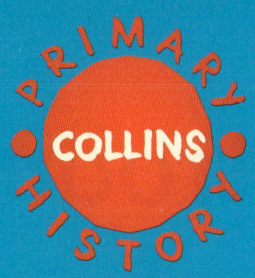

Ancient Egypt

RICHARD WORSNOP

Contents

	Page
Introduction	2
The Pharaohs	5
The Last Rulers	8
The Gods	10
Death	14
Great Builders	19
Tutankhamun	23
The River Nile	26
Farming and Trade	28
Workers and Slaves	30
Homes	32
Costume and Make-up	35
Writing	38

Introduction

The people you will read about in this book lived thousands of years ago. They lived in the country of Egypt which is in North Africa. We call them the **Ancient** Egyptians because they lived such a very long time ago.

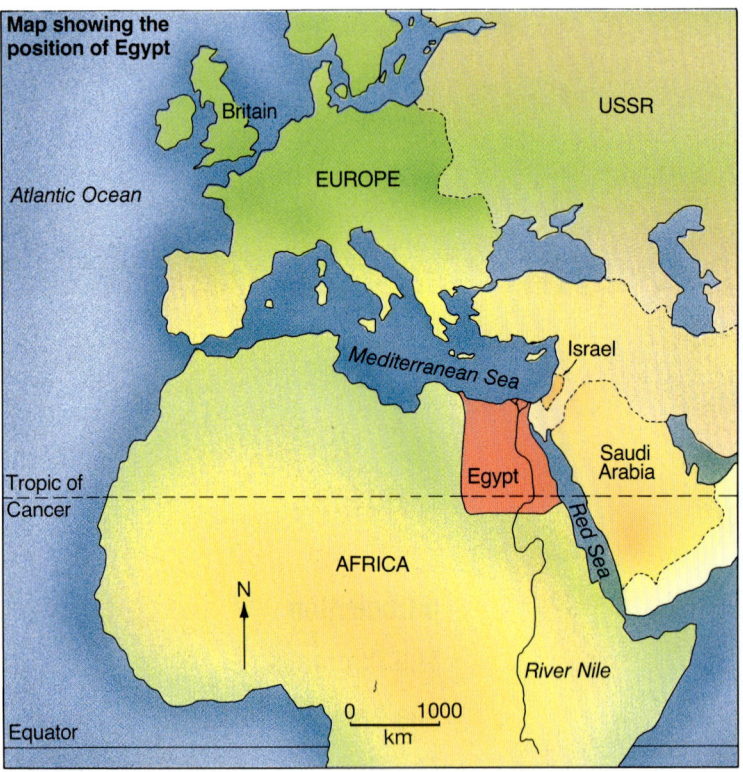

Many of their buildings and temples can still be seen, even though some of them were built over four thousand years ago.

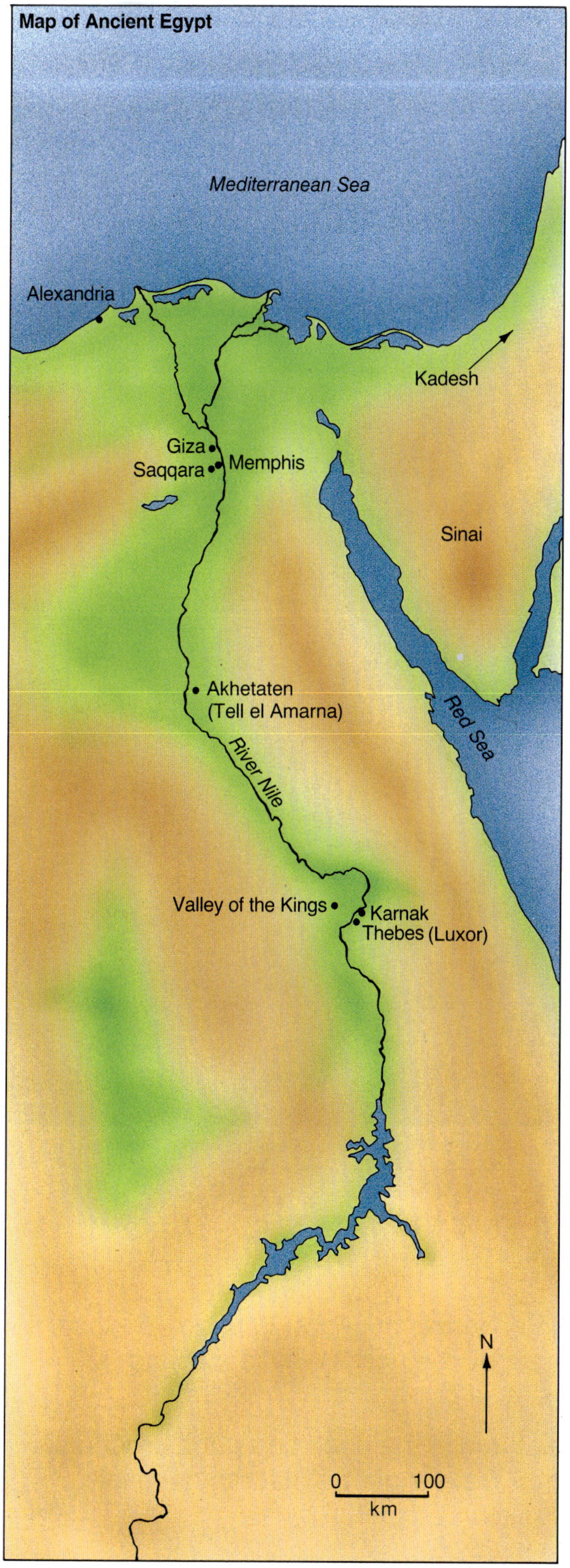

Map of Ancient Egypt

The Ancient Egyptians lived on the banks of the River Nile, with the dry desert all around them.

This map shows some of the important places in Ancient Egypt which you will read about in this book. The capital of Ancient Egypt was, at first, Memphis, but it was later moved to Thebes.

How do we know about these people who lived such a very long time ago?

Archaeologists have studied the statues, paintings and writing they left behind. They have also discovered the **tombs** of rich Egyptians. Inside the tombs they have found furniture, games, books and even chariots. This means that we can learn a lot about the Ancient Egyptian **civilisation**.

▶ An archaeologist looking at Egyptian writing.

ACTIVITIES

1. The Nile is the only river in Egypt. Why do you think all the towns are by the river? Why is the land green near the river?

2. Look at the pictures in the book and get a brochure on Egypt from a Travel Agent. What do you think the weather is like in Egypt?

The Pharaohs

The Egyptians wrote that Egypt was once two separate countries. A strong king came and made the two countries join together in about 2920 **BC**. No-one wrote about it at the time so we are not sure of what happened.

This strong king became the first ruler of Egypt. He was the first **pharaoh**. After him there were hundreds of pharaohs. They ruled Egypt for about three thousand years.

The pharaoh was very important. The Ancient Egyptians believed that he was a god. This made him very powerful.

The pharaoh sometimes wore a special crown with a cobra on it. The cobra was a goddess who protected the pharaoh. The Egyptians believed that the snake could spit poisonous fire at the pharaoh's enemies.

The pharaoh had to be strong and clever to rule Egypt well and to keep peace. He had to control his enemies in other countries and needed a good army.

▶ A ruler holding his enemy by the hair.

If the pharaoh was weak or foolish he found it hard to rule. Some pharaohs stayed in power for a very short time. At other times there was a lot of fighting and no proper ruler.

One pharaoh, called Hatshepsut, was a woman but she called herself 'King'. She often wore men's clothes and a false beard.

Rameses II became pharaoh in 1290 BC. He had to fight Egypt's enemies, the Hittites. In 1285 BC his army fought The Battle of Kadesh in Syria. Egyptian writers said that the gods gave Rameses a great victory. The Hittites wrote a different story. Probably, neither side really won the battle. Several years later peace was made between the two sides.

Rameses ruled until 1224 BC and he kept Egypt's enemies under control.

He built more temples than any other pharaoh. The walls of the temples were filled with stories of his 'greatness'.

▲ A pharaoh in battle against his enemies.

ACTIVITIES

1 Why do you think we know so little about early Egyptian history?

2 Draw a picture or make a model of the pharaoh's crown showing the snake.

See if you can find different pictures of pharaohs' crowns and draw them. Did they always wear the same crowns?

3 What different things helped to make a pharaoh powerful?

4 Why do you think Hatshepsut called herself 'King' and wore men's clothes?

5 Read these three sentences.
   a) Rameses was an Egyptian pharaoh.
   b) Rameses won a great victory.
   c) Rameses was a great pharaoh.

Are all the sentences definitely true? Which is an opinion?

The Last Rulers

The pharaohs ruled Egypt for thousands of years. Then Egypt grew weak. It was attacked by other countries.

First the Persian soldiers attacked Egypt. Then the Greek soldiers **invaded.** Their leader was called Alexander The Great. Alexander was popular in Egypt. He went to the temples and was called pharaoh. He ordered a beautiful city to be built and called it Alexandria.

In 323 BC Alexander died and his friend Ptolemy ruled Egypt. The Ptolemy family ruled Egypt for about three hundred years.

Ptolemy.

Cleopatra

A queen called Cleopatra was the last of the Ptolemy family to rule Egypt. She tried hard to stop her country from being taken by the Romans.

Cleopatra was meant to be very beautiful. Two of Rome's most powerful men fell in love with her. The first was Julius Caesar. A Roman writer called Plutarch tells the story of when Cleopatra wanted to meet Caesar. She was carried into his house, wrapped inside a carpet which she gave to him as a present.

▲ Coin showing Cleopatra.

Later Caesar was killed. Cleopatra fell in love with his friend, Antony. They wanted to rule Egypt together. Rome attacked them and there was a great sea battle. Cleopatra's navy lost.

Antony killed himself but Cleopatra was captured by the Roman leader Augustus. Augustus wanted to take her back to Rome to show the people the great queen he had beaten.

Cleopatra decided to kill herself. One story says she let a poisonous snake bite her. Plutarch, the writer, says.

The truth of the matter no-one knows.

Egypt became part of the Roman Empire. There were no more pharaohs.

ACTIVITIES

1. Do you think the coin showing Cleopatra gives us a good idea of what she looked like? Do you think she was beautiful?

2. Why do you think Cleopatra killed herself?

3. This coin was made by Augustus. It says 'Aegypto Capta'. What do you think these words mean? Why did he choose a picture of a crocodile?

9

The Gods

The Egyptians believed in many different gods. Some were well known. Others were only worshipped in certain towns. The Egyptians thought their gods sometimes disguised themselves as animals and birds when they came to earth.

This **tomb** picture shows two gods. The ram headed god is Chnum. He was god of creation. The other god has a bird's head. He was Thoth, god of writers. He is making marks on a stick to show how long the new baby will live.

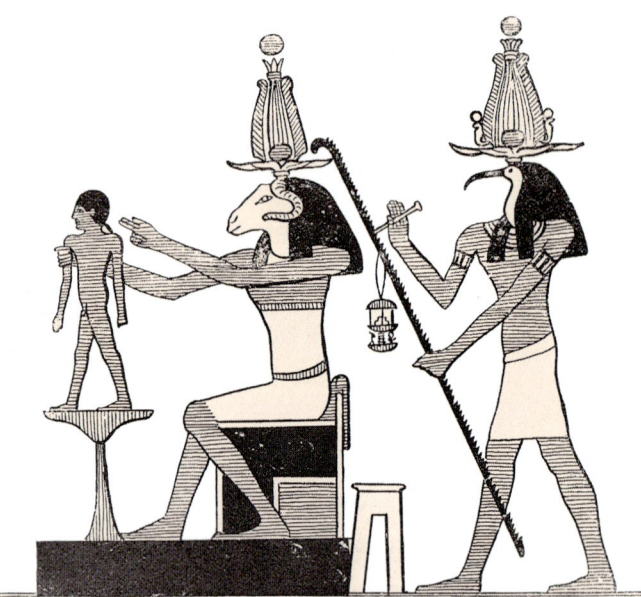

▶ Chnum and Thoth.

Another important god was Sobek, the crocodile god. He was god of water.

▶ Sobek.

Priests and Temples

Temples were built for the gods. Some were very large and important buildings. The Egyptians believed that the gods lived in the temples and that the pharaoh could go and visit them there.

▲ The temple at Karnak.

It was the job of the priests to look after the temples. They took gifts to the gods and said prayers and hymns. On important religious days the pharaoh visited the gods himself. Ordinary people were not allowed into the god's **sanctuary** in the temple to worship with the priests and pharaoh.

One God

> When you rise in the eastern horizon
> You fill every land with your beauty
> You are beautiful, great, splendid!

This is part of a poem to the sun god written by pharaoh Akhenaten. Archaeologists found it on the walls of his tomb. Akhenaten ruled Egypt from about 1353 to 1335 BC.

Akhenaten.

Akhenaten believed in one god who created the world. He called this god the sun god, Aten.

He ordered all the people and priests in Egypt not to pray to any other gods. The old temples were closed.

Akhenaten had a new city built for himself and his god. He built temples for Aten with no roofs. He lived in his new city with his wife, Nefertiti.

Akhenaten and Nefertiti.

But the priests hated Akhenaten. There were attacks by enemies from other countries. Akhenaten could not keep control of the country.

No-one knows how Akhenaten died; perhaps he was poisoned by one of his relatives. After he died people went back to praying to their old gods. The new city and the temples were pulled down.

Magic

Ordinary people only celebrated the important gods on special feast days. They did not go into the temples.

Magic was very important to all Egyptians. There were magic books, magic spells and magical days which brought good or bad luck. There were many famous magicians. One book told people what their dreams meant.

> If a man sees himself in a dream:
> eating donkey flesh, good, it means his promotion,
> looking into a deep well, bad, it means being put in prison,
> eating an egg, bad, his belongings will be taken away.

ACTIVITIES

1 What is Chnum doing in the picture on page 10?

2 When do you think was the special time for praying to Sobek?

3 Why do you think the priests hated Akhenaten?

4 In the picture of Akhenaten and Nefertiti, what are the most important things in the picture? Why did Akhenaten build temples with no roofs?

5 Draw pictures or make models of some of the gods. Find pictures of more Egyptian gods and draw or model them.

6 This is the design of an Egyptian necklace to keep people safe.

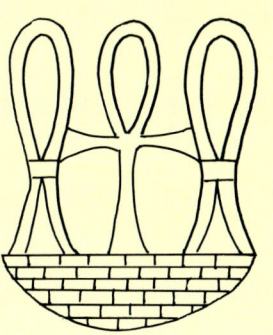

It is made up of three Egyptian symbols:

all   life   protection

Make the necklace out of card and hang it round your neck.

Death

The Journey to Heaven

When Egyptians died they believed that they had to make a long journey to heaven. They wanted to live for ever in the company of Osiris, god and king of the dead.

This is a book of magic spells called 'A Book of the Dead'. It belonged to a man called Nakht. Archaeologists have found many books like this in Egyptian **tombs**. They were to help dead people find their way to heaven.

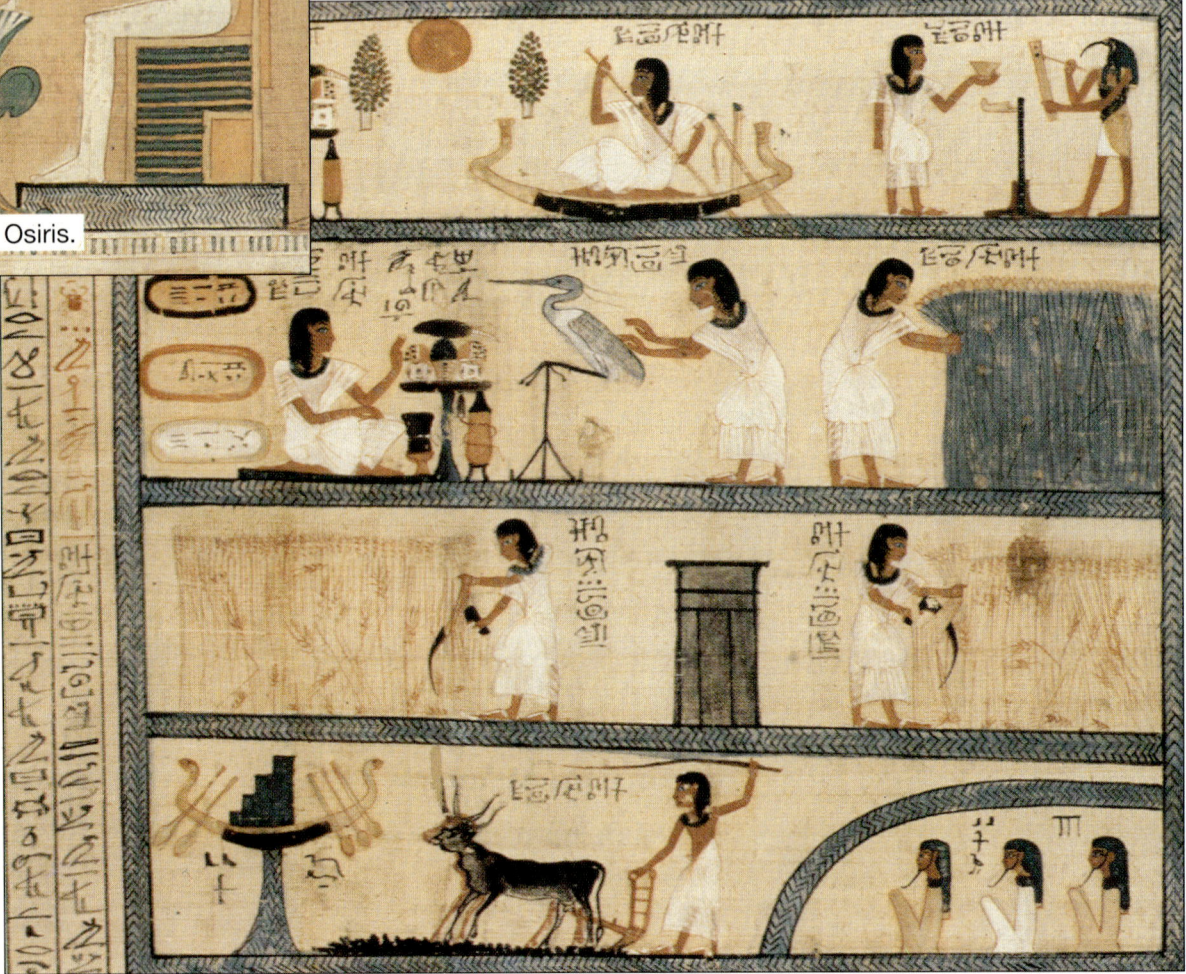

Osiris.

The first picture shows Nakht in his boat rowing across to the Field of Rushes (heaven). Then he prays to a magic bird. Other pictures show what he hopes he will be able to do in heaven.

The journey to heaven had many dangers. There was a giant serpent, a monkey with a trap, a hot furnace and a very hungry crocodile.

Nakht's book also had a spell against the monsters.

Get back! Get away from me! Stay away you evil one! Do not come against me. Do not live upon my magic. . . . No crocodile who lives on magic will take it away from me.

At the end of the journey there was the last test. This picture shows a man being judged before being allowed into heaven.

Anubis, god of funerals, weighed the heart against the feather of truth. People were asked questions about the bad things they had done. If they told lies the heart weighed more than the feather. Then the heart was thrown to the monster, Ammit. The name Ammit means 'Gobbler up of the Dead'.

15

Mummies

To make the journey to heaven the Egyptians believed they needed their bodies. If their bodies went rotten they could not get to heaven.

Bodies had to be preserved. For about two thousand years the Egyptians tried different ways to stop the dead bodies rotting. By about 2600 BC they had found a way.

The bodies were taken to a House of the Dead where they were mummified by **embalmers**. The Greek writer, Herodotus, visited Egypt in about 455 BC. He wrote about the work of the embalmers and how the **mummy** was made.

> They take first an iron hook and with it draw out the brain through the nostrils . . . and take out the whole contents of the stomach which they then clean, washing it with palm wine . . . after that they fill the hole with myrrh and other spices . . . and sew up the opening. Then the body is placed in natron for seventy days. It is washed and wrapped round, from head to foot with bandages of fine linen cloth smeared with gum . . .

▼ Mask of an Egyptian princess.

The natron (a kind of salt) was very important to dry the body up. Archaeologists have found bodies wrapped in 375 square metres of linen. The head of the body was covered with a mask to show what the person looked like when they were alive. The masks of rich people were gilded with gold.

After mummification the body was put into a coffin.

Rich people's **tombs** were covered in paintings. They were supposed to be magic. The Egyptians believed the pictures would come alive. Then the dead person could do all the things they liked doing when they were alive.

Before the ghost of the person could start the journey to heaven the priest had to perform a ceremony. It was called 'Opening the mouth'. The priest touched the mouth, ears, nose and eyes saying –

> You live again, you live again forever.

▲ Mummy and coffin.

▼ Opening the mouth ceremony.

17

Some bodies have been found which were preserved because the Egyptians buried them in the hot, dry sand. The body below is called Ginger because he still has a little ginger hair.

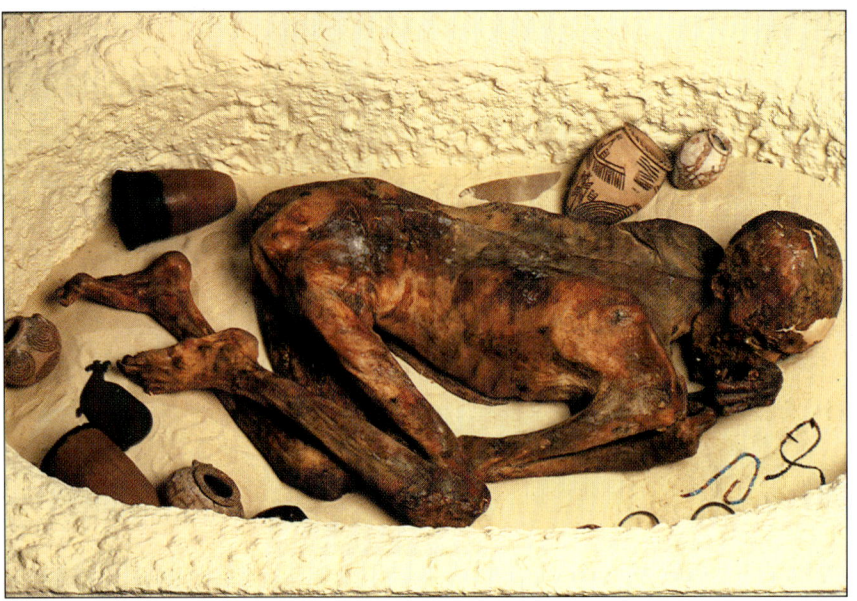

ACTIVITIES

1 Ammit was part lion, part crocodile and part hippopotamus. Why do you think the Egyptians used these animals for this god?

2 Draw the monster from Nakht's spell on page 15.

3 Tell the story of a journey to heaven. Remember the boat, all the dangers and the final test.

4 Imagine you are watching the embalmers. Write about what you see, smell and hear.

5 Paint pictures for the wall of a tomb showing what you would like to do in heaven.

6 Do you think the man buried in the sand is rich or poor? Do you think he was buried before or after the Egyptians had learnt about mummies?

Great Builders

Pyramids were built as tombs for the pharaohs. One of the first large stone pyramids was the Step Pyramid at Saqquara. It was built about 2620 BC as the tomb of a pharaoh called Djoser.

About ninety years later the Egyptians built a new kind of pyramid.

The Great Pyramid was built for the pharaoh Cheops at Giza. It is the biggest pyramid and is 146 metres high. It is made of about two million blocks of limestone, each weighing about 2500 kilograms.

Herodotus learnt about the pyramids when he visited Egypt. He wrote about how the Egyptians built them.

▲ The Step Pyramid.

> Some dragged stones from the quarries . . . to the Nile; the stones were taken across the river in boats . . . They worked in gangs of 100 000 men . . . It took 20 years to build the pyramid.

▶ The Great Pyramid.

The pharaohs were buried in the pyramids with treasures, pictures and objects to help them in the next world. The pyramids often had cleverly built passages inside them with dead ends and false doors.

▶ Scarab beetles with jewels were sometimes buried with the pharaoh.

Robbers

Robbers knew about the many treasures and broke into the pyramids to steal the jewels and gold. Around 1550 BC, the pharaohs decided to hide their tombs so thieves could not find them. The tombs were built deep into the sides of a secret valley in Thebes (Luxor), the Valley of the Kings. Robbers still managed to break into the new tombs. This is one robber's confession.

> Then we found . . . the mummy of the king . . . his head had a mask of gold . . . its coverings were all gold and silver . . . We stripped off all the gold and the ornaments and the covering. We found the queen . . . then set fire to the coffins. We divided the booty and made the gold ornaments and covering into eight parts.

Statues

The Egyptians also built statues. They were often carved from one huge block of stone.

This is a statue of an Egyptian **sphinx**. The sphinx was a god with the head of a man and the body of a lion. Sphinxes often had the head of a pharaoh and they were used to protect the pyramids.

▶ Sphinx at Memphis, built about 1500 BC.

These tomb pictures show men working on different statues.

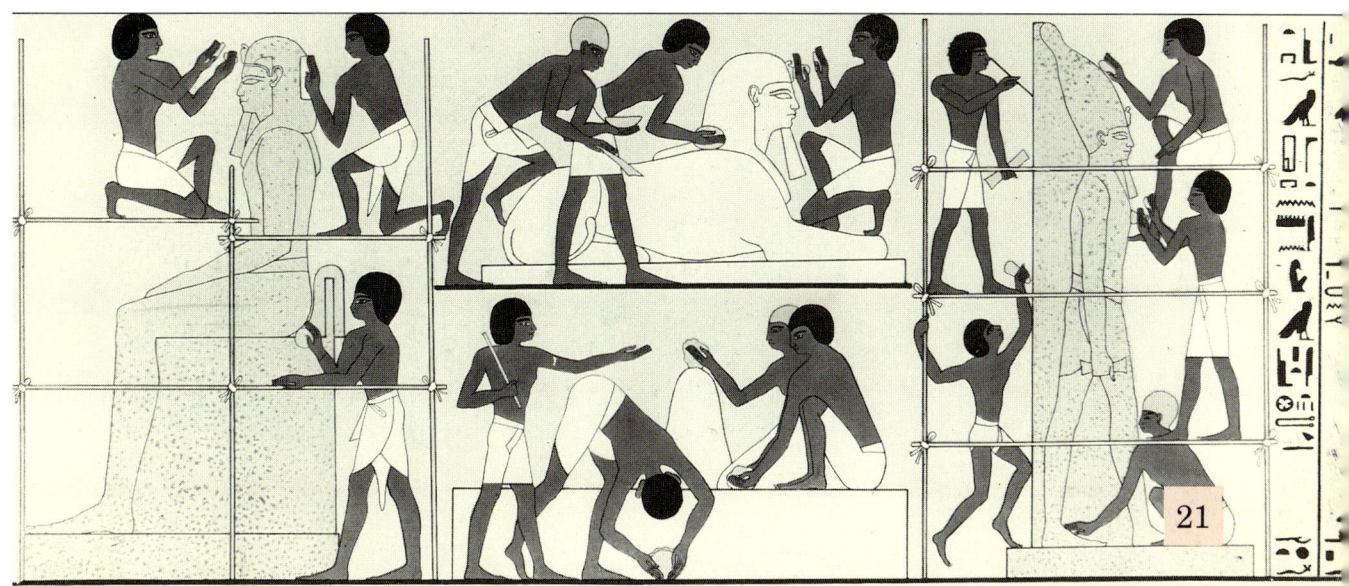

ACTIVITIES

1. What is the difference between the Step Pyramid and the Great Pyramid?

2. How do you think the huge stones were moved? What problems would there have been with so many people working for such a long time in the desert?

3. Why do you think the Egyptians stopped burying their pharaohs in pyramids? Do you think there was more than one reason?

4. Imagine you were one of the robbers. How did you steal the gold and jewels? Write about entering the pyramid, the dark passages, finding the room with the mummy and dividing the jewels.

5. Look at the pictures on the last page. What are the men doing? How did they reach the top of the statues?

6. Can you build a model of a pyramid, or make a sphinx from clay or plasticine?

7. Herodotus wrote about the building of the Great Pyramid about two thousand years after it was built. Do you believe it took a hundred thousand men and twenty years to build? Can you be sure?

Tutankhamun

Tutankhamun was a **pharaoh** who ruled Ancient Egypt for ten years. He was nine years old when he became pharaoh and was married straight away to Nefertiti's third daughter. In 1323 BC he was buried in The Valley of the Kings, near Thebes.

In 1922 an archaeologist called Howard Carter found the **tomb** of the pharaoh, Tutankhamun.

Carter and Lord Carnarvon had searched for the tomb for many years. In November 1922 Carter and his workers cleared some huts which had been used by Ancient Egyptian builders. They dug underneath these huts and found some steps, leading to an entrance. At the end of a corridor, Carter found a blocked doorway, stamped with Tutankhamun's seal. He wrote in his diary:

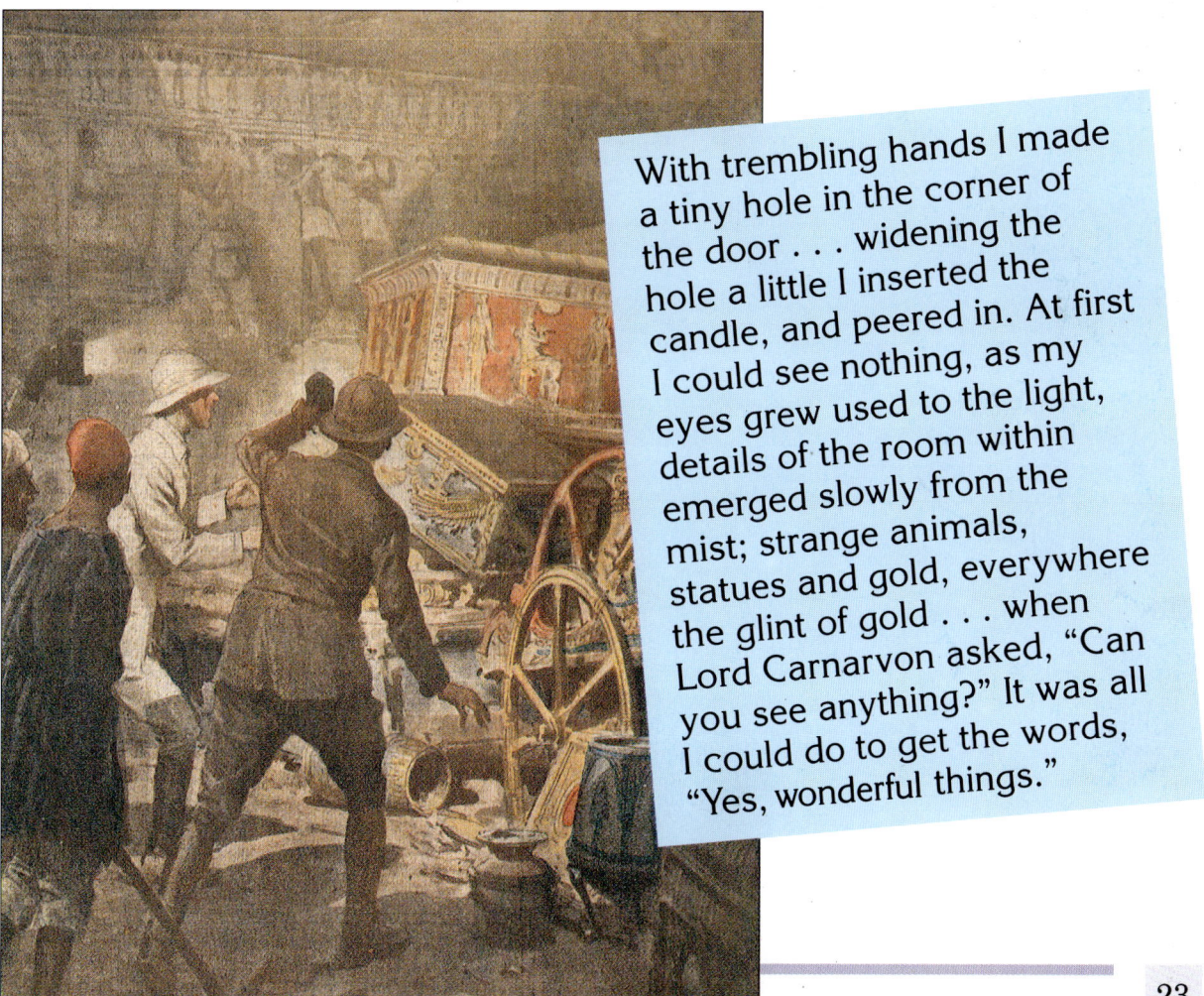

▼ A painting of Carter's discovery.

With trembling hands I made a tiny hole in the corner of the door . . . widening the hole a little I inserted the candle, and peered in. At first I could see nothing, as my eyes grew used to the light, details of the room within emerged slowly from the mist; strange animals, statues and gold, everywhere the glint of gold . . . when Lord Carnarvon asked, "Can you see anything?" It was all I could do to get the words, "Yes, wonderful things."

23

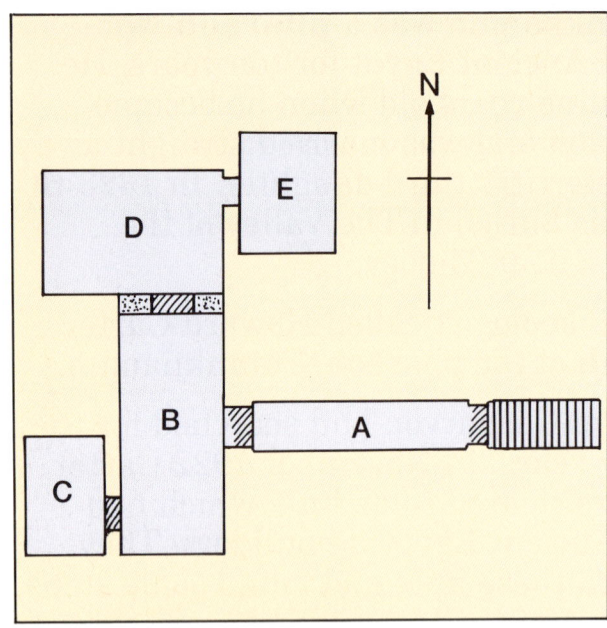

Carter found that the corridor (A) was filled with rubble. In room B he found three animal-headed couches, four chariots and other treasures.

The small room (C) contained a jumble of beds, chairs, stools and boxes.

It was in the burial room (D) that Carter found the mummy of pharaoh Tutankhamun. It was inside a coffin which was made of solid gold and weighed 134 kilograms.

In the treasury (E) Carter discovered many carved wooden figures and golden treasures.

▼ Carter looking at the mummy of Tutankhamun and the coffin after cleaning.

Carter found a bunch of dried flowers on the floor and a fingerprint where someone had touched some wet paint.

Before anything was moved it had to be drawn and photographed. Guards were outside the tomb to stop robbers.

▲ Detail of throne, showing Tutankhamun and his queen.

▶ Vulture collar worn by Tutankhamun.

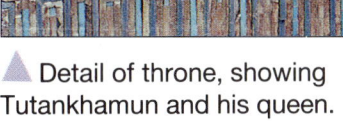

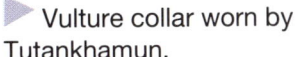

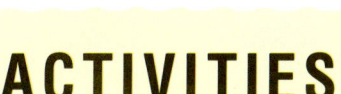

▲ Gold plated throne.

ACTIVITIES

1 Carter was the first person in the tomb for three thousand years. How do you think he felt? Write about the discovery as if you were Carter.

2 Robbers had been in the tomb thousands of years before Carter found it. The robbers did not take much. Can you think why? What do you think happened to them?

3 Draw a picture or make a model of Tutankhamun's coffin.

The River Nile

Every year between June and October the River Nile flooded its banks. The farmers' fields were under water for about three months. It left behind rich soil which made the land fertile.

When the Greek writer, Herodotus, visited Egypt in about 455 BC he wrote:

> When the Nile overflows, the country is converted into a sea, and nothing appears but the cities, which look like islands.

The Egyptians made the river into this god called Hapy.

An Egyptian priest wrote this hymn.

▼ The god Hapy.

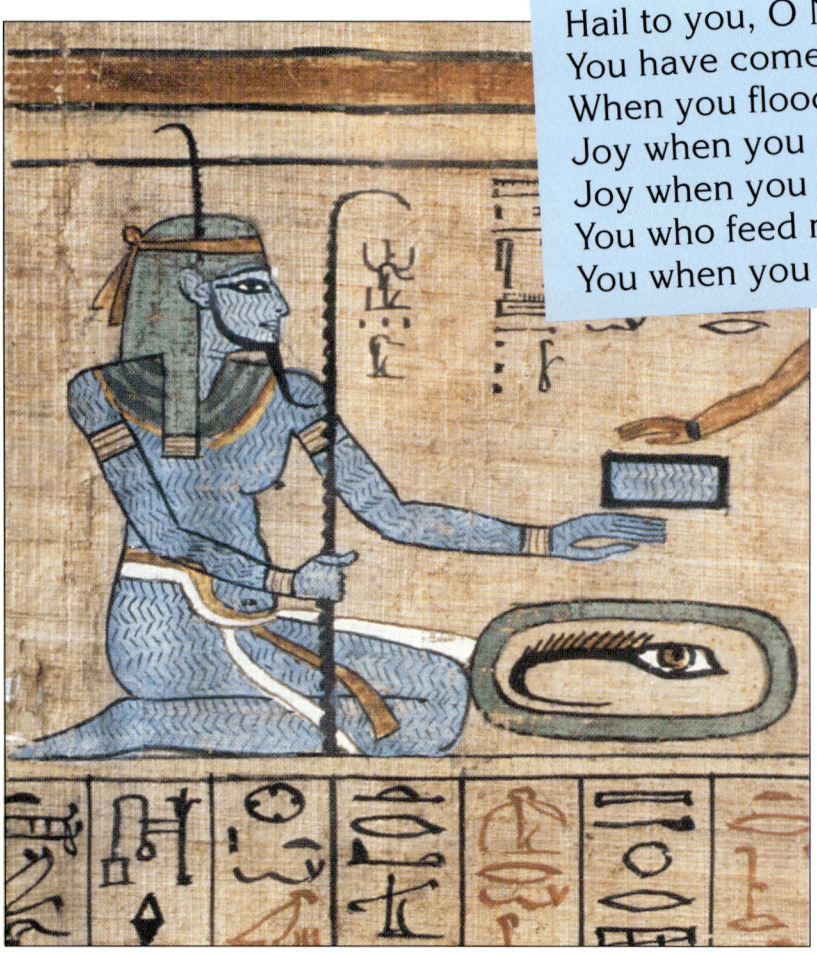

> Hail to you, O Nile! . . .
> You have come to feed Egypt . . .
> When you flood the land rejoices . . .
> Joy when you come, O Nile!
> Joy when you come!
> You who feed men and animals . . .
> You when you come!

The priests in Egypt were also important because they could forecast when the floods would come. Each year they watched the level of the river water. They marked special measures for the water level in the rocks on the river banks. These were called Nilometers.

The Nilometers showed how high the floods would be. Very low water meant a poor harvest. Very high measurements meant deep floods which would damage buildings, fields and water channels.

A Roman called Pliny visited Egypt. He measured the rise of the river in 'ells'. An ell was about one and a half metres. Pliny said:

> A rise of twelve ells meant hunger.
> A rise of thirteen meant suffering.
> A rise of fourteen meant happiness.
> A rise of fifteen meant security.
> A rise of eighteen meant disaster.

ACTIVITIES

1 Herodotus wrote that Egypt was the gift of the Nile. What did he mean?

2 What measurement of ells would the Egyptians hope for each year? What would this measurement be in metres? What kind of disaster would a rise of eighteen ells bring?

3 Read the story of the pharaoh's dreams of plenty and famine in Genesis Chapter 41, in the Bible. What measurements do you think the priests found in the first seven years and in the second seven years?

Farming and Trade

After the flooding of the Nile had gone down the crops were planted. The Egyptians grew corn and barley to make bread and beer, and flax to make linen. The **harvesting** began in spring and was finished by May.

Harvesting crops (right).

Harvesting grapes (below).

Egypt also produced wine and oil. In this picture men are harvesting grapes and making wine.

Herodotus wrote:

> Their drink is a wine they obtain from barley, as they have no vines in their country.

Men also hunted wild birds by the river, kept cattle and fished in the Nile.

▶ Fish in the River Nile.

The Nile was always full of different kinds of boats. Smaller boats carried people and the bigger boats carried cattle, grain and stones.

The bigger boats did **trade** with other countries. The Egyptians bought wood to make their boats, metals, ivory, gold and animals such as giraffes and leopards for their skins.

▲ Little model boats like these have been found in Egyptian tombs.

ACTIVITIES

1 Look at both pictures on page 28 and describe what is happening.

2 Was Herodotus right about the wine? What kind of 'wine' is made from barley? Can we believe everything he wrote?

3 The Egyptians could not travel everywhere on the river. How do you think they travelled on the land?

4 Look at the picture of the River Nile on page 3 and at the model of the boat on this page. Draw a picture of Ancient Egyptian boats on the Nile.

Workers and Slaves

Rich people owned large houses and farms. They had workers and servants to do the work in the fields and in the house.

▶ Ploughing the fields.

▶ Preparing bread.

These workers were often paid in jugs of beer, loaves of bread or sacks of corn. Poor families worked in the big farms but often had their own small houses nearby. Poor men and women shared the work in the fields. At home they baked bread, brewed beer and made their own clothes. Poor people also had to spend some time every year working for the pharaoh, building temples and tombs.

Rich people often bought **slaves** to work for them. The slaves were not paid, they were owned by the rich people and were not allowed to leave.

An Egyptian writes that in about 1275 BC a woman called Iritnofret went to the court.

> The merchant Reia came to me with the Syrian slave, who was still a girl, and he said to me, 'Buy this girl and pay for her.' . . . I took the girl and paid him her price.

Prisoners who had been captured in battle were made into slaves. They were made to work in the quarries and the gold mines in the desert. Sometimes they were blinded or **branded**.

ACTIVITIES

1 The Egyptians did not think it was wrong to buy and own another person? What do you think?

2 Iritnofret bought the slave on her own. Maybe she did not even ask her husband about it. What does that tell you about some rich women in Egypt?

3 Why do you think some slaves were blinded or branded?

4 Read about Joseph in the Bible (Genesis 37, verse 25). Who sold Joseph to the Egyptians as a slave? You could read the rest of Joseph's story and act it out.

Homes

This was once a village where workers who built and painted the tombs lived. The **ruins** help to show us the kind of homes poor people lived in. Each house was about six metres long. There were seventy houses in the village.

▶ Deir el Medina, a workman's village at Luxor.

Rich people often had two houses – one in the town and one in the country. Large houses often had bathrooms. People stood in a stone basin and poured water over themselves. Archaeologists have found some homes which had toilets with stone seats.

Egyptian houses were normally made of mud bricks baked in the hot sun.

▶ These model houses were found in Egyptian tombs.

32

This chair and bed were found in Egyptian tombs.

Gardens

In the larger houses vines were grown in the garden. Fruit and vegetables were also grown. Water was stored in a pool and a shaduf was used to lift the water out. The shaduf had a heavy stone at one end and a bucket at the other.

Animals were also kept. The most popular were oxen and sheep. But there were also goats, pigs and donkeys.

◀ Shadufs are still used today in some parts of Egypt.

Women

Women were important people in the house. **Tomb** pictures show rich women receiving presents or watching over the work. Poorer women were often servants and pictures show them making bread and beer, spinning and weaving. Only royal women could become powerful.

33

Food

The Egyptians ate fish, cheese, bread and fruit. The rich people also ate meat. Beer was the most popular drink.

Rich people had servants to prepare their food. They had big dinner parties where dancing girls and musicians entertained them. Food for a big dinner could include a goose, the head of an ox, loaves of bread, grapes, figs, fruits, a bag of spices and jars of wine.

▶ Dancing girls at a dinner party.

ACTIVITIES

1 Look at the models of Egyptian houses on page 32. Which would be a rich family's home and which would be a poor family's home? Why do you think they had flat roofs?

2 Look at the chair and the bed. Do they look comfortable? Do you think poor people had furniture like this?

3 Shadufs are still used in Egypt today. Has everything else in Egypt stayed the same? Does the Nile still flood every year? What do you think has changed?

4 Design a menu for an Egyptian banquet.

Costume and Make-up

This **mummy** coffin is an Egyptian lady. She is wearing jewellery. Her eyes have been carefully made up. She is wearing a wig.

Carvings, **tomb** pictures and mummy coffins tell us a lot about Egyptian costumes. This picture shows a man and woman wearing simple linen clothes.

Both men and women sometimes wore wigs.

This painting was found in an Egyptian tomb. Everyone has a cone on their head. No cones have been found and so what they were is a mystery. Most historians think they held perfume.

Both rich men and women wore bracelets and necklaces. Jewellery was supposed to be lucky. It kept away evil spirits. Much of the jewellery was made of gold with brightly coloured semi-precious stones or glass. Women also wore rings, girdles and anklets. Earrings became popular around 1500 BC.

Necklace.

Earrings.

Women put make-up on their cheeks, lips and around their eyes. They kept their creams and make-up in little jars like those in the picture. At the bottom of the picture is a make-up palette which women used to mix the make-up and put it on.

ACTIVITIES

1 Do you think poor people who had to work on the river or the land wore make-up and jewellery? Why?

2 From the evidence in this chapter draw a rich Egyptian lady with her wig, jewellery and make-up.

3 Look at all the pictures of people in this book. What can you learn about how the Egyptians dressed? Does all the evidence show people wearing the same clothes? What differences are there? Why do you think this is?

Writing

The Ancient Egyptians wrote in pictures. Each picture is called a **hieroglyph**. People who were taught to read and use hieroglyphs were called scribes. Only rich boys could learn to be scribes. They were taught by the priests in the temples. They had to learn more than seven hundred different signs and put them together in the right way.

A scribe.

Some signs stood for one or two of our letters, like these.

	Letter	Meaning		Letter	Meaning
	A	vulture		M	owl
	B	leg		N	water
	D	hand		P	stool
	F	viper		Q	hill
	G	pot or stand		R	mouth
	CH	rope		S	cloth
	I	reed		T	loaf
	J	serpent		W	chick
	K	basket		Y	reeds
	L	lion		Z	bolt

38

Some signs tell us about the meaning of a word.

	god		man
	leg, foot.		woman
	walking, movement.		people
	walking backwards, returning.		young, child.
	enemy (man with arms tied behind).		desert, foreign country.
	die, enemy (man lying on ground).		village, town.

Scribes used black or red ink. Their pens were made from reeds. Paper was made from the papyrus plant which grew by the River Nile. Our word 'paper' comes from the same word.

ACTIVITIES

1 Try to make up your own sentence using hieroglyphics. Can other people read it?

2 Some workmen were digging in a rubbish tip which was thousands of years old. They found hundreds of rolls of paper covered in Egyptian hieroglyphics. Discoveries like this tell us a lot about Ancient Egypt. What would people learn about the modern day from a rubbish tip?

3 The Egyptians wanted to live for ever. In one way they succeeded. We know a great deal about their civilisation from the writings, objects and buildings, even though they lived such a very long time ago. Do you think the work of the archaeologists who discovered these things is important? Would you like to be an archaeologist? What discovery would you like to make? Why?

Glossary

ancient	Something very old, from a very long time ago.
archaeologist	Someone who studies the past, usually by digging things up.
BC	Before Christ.
branded	When you brand a person or an animal you mark them so that everyone knows who owns them.
civilisation	A group of people with its own organisation, special laws, art, customs etc.
embalmers	The people who made the mummies.
harvesting	Gathering of crops.
hieroglyph	Egyptian letters.
invade	To enter a country with an army.
mummy	A dead body which has been preserved.
pharaoh	Ruler of Egypt.
pyramid	Huge, stone building built as tombs for Egyptian pharaohs.
ruins	All that is left from something which is very old or which has been destroyed.
sanctuary	The most holy part of the temple.
slaves	Peoples owned by others. They have to work for others and are not free to do what they want.
sphinx	Statues with bodies of lions and heads of people.
tomb	A building where dead people are buried.
trade	Buying and selling goods, exchanging one thing for another.